EARLESTOWN

Yesterdays of A Railway Town

Barry Carman

Earlestown Railway Station - Circa 1904

ACKNOWLEDGEMENTS

I am indebted to many people for their co-operation in preparing this publication, especially those who entrusted me with family photographs and who agreed to be interviewed which I hope brings the text to life.

I would particularly like to mention the following people - my late father who ignited the idea when he once said "Earlestown, you could write a book". Edna Sherlock and Geoff Simm for continuing to fuel my interest, Billy and Margery Kenning and Winifred Harvey for sharing their life-long memories of Earlestown and to Doug Waring for his help in so many ways.

The staff of Newton-le-Willows Library for their assistance. The staff at Willow Printing and to yourselves for purchasing a copy of the book.

Thank you.

Signed copy To Thomas and Heather

Barry Carman

27th September 1992

ISBN 0-9519509-0-8

Publisher:
B. Carman
7A London Row
NEWTON-LE-WILLOWS
Merseyside
WA12 8RY
0925 220556

Printed by:
Willow Printing
75/79 Back Cross Lane
NEWTON-LE-WILLOWS
Merseyside
WA12 9YG
0925 222449/228524

CONTENTS

COVER PHOTOGRAPHS
FRONT:
Men - Viaduct Works Bolt Shop, St. Johns Church, Edith Hornby, Garret Ronayne
BACK:
1906 Juniors Class, Earlestown District School
1890 The Grandstand, Newton Racecourse

NEWTON LE WILLOWS
EARLESTOWN
Sewage Filter Bed
Coal Screening Depot
Viaduct
Lyme Pits
Brick Works
Woodside
Swan Road
Hall House Farm
White House
Swan Inn
St. Philip's Church
Newton Common
School
Football Ground
Hazel Grove
Athletic Ground
Pavilion
Club
Wellesley House
Parish Room
Crow Lane West
Yew Tree House
Crow Lane Farm
Public Library
All Saints Church
Crow House Farm
Schools
Allotment Gardens
Recreation Ground
St. John's Mission Hall
Market Place
Heald Farm
Timber Yard
Stone
Penkford Street
Penkford Farm
Penkford Lodge
Penkford Bridge
Weir
Overflow
Spring
Sewage Works
West End Outfall
(Newton in le Willows U.D.C.)
Newton Common Lock
Swing bridge
Inn
Dingle Cottage
Earle Cottage
Earle Street
Band Stand
Pavilion
Inst
Griffin Hotel
Earlestown Junction
Warrington Junction
Biscuit Machinery Works
Viaduct Works
Sankey Hill
Sankey Viaduct
Sankey Cottages
Reservoir
Sankey Sugar Works
Mill Farm
Higher Astley
Red Brow Wood
Bleak House
Bradley Wharf
Bradley Lock
Bradley Lane
Bradlegh Wood
War Memorial Hospital
UD Bdy
Park Brow Plantation
Penkford Lane
Station
Collins Green

FOREWORD

To attempt to present Earlestown as a picturesque old world place would be a mistake. The romance of Earlestown is the romance of the Railway, the Viaduct Works and the growth of the Town.

In interpreting the physical remains of yesterday's buildings it is possible to learn a great deal about the ways in which the town was organised and its growth, but it is more interesting to feel the way back into the lives of the people who created, lived and worked in Earlestown.

If we wanted to research local history thoroughly we would have to talk to the people who were employed in 1857 in the Viaduct Smithy, the children on their first visit to the District Infants School or to Liza Lovesey as she went around the town with her horse and cart selling fruit and vegetables, but instead we have to rely largely on written records. At best, these give us facts and figures, but they rarely touch on human details that strike a chord in our own life.

For this reason, YESTERDAYS OF A RAILWAY TOWN looks back to 1853 and proceeds into a period directly remembered by some, familiar to many more but increasingly removed from today's experience of life.

Photographs are also a rewarding source of information, woven into the lives and memories of the people concerned. There is something very moving about a faded picture of Winnie Smith outside her family's cafe in Queen Street, or the Sunday School Walking Day taken in the first quarter of the century. For all its technical imperfections, it makes a far greater impact than a professional one in mint condition. It often has a powerful ability, awakening recollections otherwise forgotten. Therefore, thank you fellow Earlestonians: this book is your memorial to a vanishing age.

INTRODUCTION

"To Grandma and Grandad Carman for the happy chance of being here in the first place."

My grandparents were William and Sarah Ellen Carman and of Cheshire stock.

William was born on 1 January 1881, being the youngest of thirteen children and his father passed away before he was born. The family home was the old Baptist Chapel, Kingsley, Nr Frodsham. He had little schooling and was employed at twelve as a farm hand along with his elder brother Fred. His birth certificate shows that his mother could not read or write as she made a simple mark of a cross in place of a signature.

Sarah Ellen (nee Joinson) was born on 4 February 1879 at Bridge Lane Farm, Frodsham and was two years older than grandad. It is understood that the family farm had to be sold, so, her elder sister, aunt Em, came with uncle Israel Dimilow to Newton to be caretakers at Wargrave Parish Church. They lived in the little row of cottages in the church grounds. Uncle Israel acted as Sexton whilst grandma helped aunt Em with the cleaning. William had met Sarah on their farm whilst operating the threshing machine and decided to follow her to Newton. He took lodgings and employment as a labourer in the forge at the Viaduct Works.

William and Sarah were married at St. Johns Church, Earlestown on 20 May 1907. On returning from the wedding they took residence at 44 Birch Street on The Common.

The landlord of the houses in Birch Street, which were new at the time, gave them the choice. William chose number 44. It is remembered that William said "*Well, Sally this will do for us.*" There they lived for over fifty years until they both passed away.

My grandparents William and Sarah Ellen Carman

44 Birch Street was a two up and two down terrace house with a long paved yard and a 'privy' toilet at the bottom. It was the family home were my late father, Thomas, his two elder sisters, Lily and Gladys and younger brother Jack were all born and brought up. Educated at the Manor 'College' as they called it, played on the old Racecourse and had to conform to strict rules laid down by their father.

When the Slump came William had to leave the Viaduct Works and took employment with Arnold Roberts working on his coal cart for a wage of £1.30/- per week plus two free bags of coal. In his spare time he returned to what he loved doing best, working on a farm, this he did until he was nearly eighty years old. Apparently at seventy eight he was stripped to the waist haymaking. Some of his time was spent at Burmans Farm but his affection was to work at the Grange Farm with the Haydock Brothers. Whilst William was out from dawn till dusk, Sarah , beautifully cared for the home. `Nit white' washing, 'wholesome cooking' and her pride and joy was polishing and dusting. Despite her disability of only having one arm from birth this didn't prevent her from maintaining her standards.

The square table in the middle of the living room was first covered with a chenille cover then a white table cloth plus a newspaper to eat off!. The four table legs were protected with grandad's old stockings. They only came off for special occasions.

The long paved yard was a hive of activity. Many sheds where constructed from thrown out timber from the Viaduct Works, one to work in, one for grandad's dog, and another for his pigeons. Grandad's speciality was making wooden trucks with iron wheels. You needed muscle to push them.

As the family grew up aunty Lily and aunty Gladys went into service at Bolton. My father first worked as a 'Saturday Lad' on the Co-op cart and then became an apprentice fitter at the Vulcan Works, whilst uncle Jack became a baker at John Russells.

My father and mother, Thomas and Edith Carman shortly before their Wedding in 1941

My father and mother married in June 1941 and lived for a short time at 44 Birch Street before moving to 2 King Street.

On a Sunday morning my father would take me along with my elder brother, Geoffrey to 44 Birch Street. My earliest recollections of the visits was that grandma would give us a cream cracker but we had to eat it in the yard in case we made any crumbs.

On leaving we were given half a crown each......

Over the Years my father told me many stories about life at 44 Birch Street and Earlestown which have been the foundation of my research for this book. Here are four of them......

A TRIP TO BLACKPOOL

"My dad decided to take us on a day trip to Blackpool using his free pass from the Viaduct, on the 10.00 a.m. train.
We arrived at Earlestown Station at 8.30 a.m. just to be in good time!!
As the train arrived, he wanted to go to the toilet and went to use the station's facility. We got on board the train with mother and the train started to leave the station, dad jumped into the guard's van at the rear and completed the journey to Blackpool. When we got off the train he shouted "You've finished, you've finished" as if it was our fault he nearly missed the train. It was the last trip we had!!"

MRS FISHER'S FANLIGHT

There were a few of the lads playing in the back including Ozzie, Bronk and little Natty and we had made a "piggy" from a pick horn. We hit it and it was a "beautiful riser".

Smash, straight through Mrs. Fisher's fanlight.

"You'll pay, you'll pay", shouted Mrs. Fisher and told us of the damage done. "You've broke the fanlight, knocked a vase off the sideboard, cracked a cup on the table and hit my husband on the rug, clogging!!

We retorted "Well love, it's not made of rubber" and we all ran off. It cost us five and a tanner between us for a new fanlight."

VULCAN CENTENARY TRIP SEPTEMBER 1930

"I was 16 years of age in 1930 when it was the Vulcan Centenary Trip to Blackpool. My mother had bought me a new cap and dad obtained a good overcoat for me for five shillings from a man who worked on the gas producer in the Viaduct. Wah - I felt a toff.

As I was walking down Market Street and arrived at the Rams Head my dad turned the corner from Earle Street. We met head on, and I was smoking my head off. He then chased me all the way back to 44 Birch Street. We did three laps around the yard and I ran to the station and just caught the train."

This photograph shows Tom at Blackpool wearing his new cap and overcoat.

About this time he got his nickname 'Slim'

OUR LIL'S WEDDING

"Our Lil married Walter Scholes on September 17th, 1932. It was quite a posh affair, full wreath and veil. Our Gladys, Ethel Edwards and Walter's cousin stood for them. The service was at St. Johns Church and the cost was 9s 7d. When we got back from the church we had a good spread. Stocking tops where off the table legs that day!!!"

Our Lil's Wedding Photograph and account from St. Johns Church

Earlestown Parish Church.

(St. John the Baptist).

Wedding Fees, etc.

Mr. Scholes

Date Sept. 17th 1932

	£	s.	d.
Publication of Banns ...		–	–
Marriage by Banns ...		4	6
Marriage by Licence ...		–	–
Certificate of Marriage ...		2	7
Verger's Services ...		2	6
Use of Organ ..		–	–
		9	7

Received by E. W. Stowe

Vicar

Date Sept. 17. 32

EARLY DAYS
circa 1840

Adapted from Mr. Cole's notes.

"Our meander starts at the junction of Crow Lane and Cross Lane which was a narrow and zig-zag lane, with a little island of land between the roads and a large pit on the roadside; on the left-hand side (towards Earlestown), there were also two large pits.

On the right-hand side was the land on which Compensation Cottages were built in 1852.

After passing the street in which Fairclough's Warehouse (known as Junction Warehouse) was erected, we should cross over the Haydock Colliery Mineral Line, on this level the bridge was not then constructed, nor were there any houses on the right hand side. On the left we are close to The Newton Workhouse and the draw well in a garden on the opposite side of the road. That would be before Bridge Street was so named, and altered to run in a straight line. In 1868 the Commissioners fixed a windlass to the well for the use of the public and very soon afterward they erected a pump.

About this time the Poor Law Guardians gave up their control over the Workhouse and it was used by the Warrington Board of Guardians under the Guardianship of Mr. William Rigby. In 1852 the premises were sold and converted into eight cottages. They were later demolished in 1885.

Proceeding down Pepper Alley (the section now known as Bridge Street), we then would come to the road (Queen Street) leading to Warrington Junction Station; the Rams Head Inn was not built, nor was there a Market Street. All around were fields, and on our way to the New Earlestown Railway Station (then called Warrington Junction Station) we should pass Chemical Street which crossed the railway on the level to the Vitriol Works. On a triangular piece of ground adjoining the present entrance to the station we would see an old white-timbered beer-house known as the Rams Head, kept by James Foster who met the trains with refreshments. He later built a public house, in Pepper Alley, since rebuilt (as we see it today) which was then also used as a farmhouse of the same name. Mr. Foster also erected the Railway Inn (known at that time as the Junction Inn) opposite the station for his son John.

Circa 1840

Earlestown Station is the building on the right.

The half timbered building is the Rams Head and the traffic is passing over Chemical Street

The station had been opened by the Grand Junction and Liverpool and Manchester Railway Companies. The fine Station Building was built circa 1839 by Thomas Stone.

On returning to Pepper Alley (Earle Street) we should come to a gentlemen's house (afterwards the old Griffin Inn), where lived Mr. John Jones, a member of the firm Jones and Potts, owner of the Viaduct Foundry. Between his home and the works was a large pit, called the fish pond.

Below the Viaduct Foundry was two small houses with garden and croft, and at the farm on the hill lived old Richard Fazackerley. This farmhouse which stood close to the roadside, was later pulled down and formed the site for Earle Cottage, where Mr. James Watson Emmett, Superintendent of the Viaduct Works, lived for many years.

The land north of Pepper Alley was part of Heald Farm occupied by Jane Meredith, and is described on the 1839 tithe map as:

NEWTON TITHE MAP 1839
OWNER THOMAS LEGH ESQ
OCCUPIER JANE MEREDITH - HEALD FARM

TITHE NO	FIELD
933	LONG FIELD
934	CROFT
936	CROFT WORTH HILL
937	ROUGH AND DINGLE
938	GARDEN
944	COMMON CLOSE
950	GREEN HEYES MEADOW
951	GREEN HEYES PART OF
1004	FOUR ACRE
1005	DIEDENS CLOSE
1006	TAYLORS CLOSE
1017	THREE ACRE
1018	LITTLE FIELD
1019	HIGHER FIELD
1020	LONG FIELD

Proceeding along Wharf Road and passing on our left the Sankey Viaduct, and on our right Stephenson's Cottage, further on was the site of Newton Common Pit then we should come into Common Road, (called St. Helens Turnpike Road), the Toll Bar being the other side of Penkford Bridge, and there we would see the Racecourse.

If it happened to be race day, you could enter on the course for it was never fenced and see the races being run, mixing with a motley crowd and sharing in the pleasures provided for the people. We should admire the imposing Grand-stand and the fashionable people thereon and notice the other smaller stands adjoining.

We could take refreshments just off the course at The Swan with Two Necks Hotel, kept by James Smiley. Before departing, we might take a stroll down The Grange and on the far side of the common we would be told that the houses are called The White Cottage, The Red House and The White House.

Returning from the Common, past the site of the Manor School, we should notice a large pit and another one on the same side coming eventually to Yew Tree Farm, where Mr. Muspratt's bailiff (Mr. Marsh) resided. In later days Mr. James Hopwood and Mr. James Pearce trained their race horses there. Vista Road was then an occupation road called High Marsh Lane.

The Haydock Colliery Mineral Line which ran from Haydock Colliery passed over Crow Lane and to Liverpool and Manchester Railway with a further line to the Racecourse. On the left we would see the Colliery line to Crow Lane Yard just behind the hedge in "Sunnyside". The right hand side of Crow Lane is the area of land which became known as "Lunts Wood" and Crow Lane Farm was used as stables for Sir John Gerrard's racehorses.

We are now back at the starting point of our pleasant and picturesque walk".

SIR HARDMAN EARLE
1792 - 1877

Hardman Earle, fourth son of Mr. Thomas Earle of Spekelands, was born on 11 July 1792. He was educated at a school near Warrington kept by a Mr. Lloyd and went to Charterhouse School, still at that time situated in Charterhouse Square in London under the Headmaster Dr. Raine. In 1822, along with his brother William, he became a partner in the firm Earles and Carter, the seed crushing firm founded in 1800.

Hardman was a man of ceaseless energy, and his business life was active and untiring; but over and above his pursuit of this he had numerous other general occupations. Liverpool knew him as a leading spirit in her politics, as an ardent supporter of her institutions and a willing worker of her charities and trusts. It is with the invention of the railway that Sir Hardman's name is most generally associated as one of its original supporters and pioneers.

There is a legend that when George Stephenson and his friends were still struggling with many difficulties and against great opposition at the commencement of their work on the celebrated Liverpool and Manchester Railway Line, Hardman Earle, then a young man, walked out one day along the whole route from Liverpool, to judge for himself of its prospects; divining its great success, he returned home to sell his shares in the water companies and invested every penny in the railway. He joined the Board of Directors of the Liverpool to Manchester Railway which was projected by his friend, Joseph Saunders and his relative Mr. Charles Lawrence was the first chairman.

Sir Hardman was one of the promoters of the Grand Junction Railway and its amalgamations to the London North-Western Railway Company. At the time of his death he was still a Director being then the oldest railway Director living.

SIR HARDMAN EARLE 1792 - 1877
FOUNDER OF EARLESTOWN

He married on 24th August 1819, Mary Langton of Kirkham. In spite of being a family man, he frequently made time for sport, both as a young man and late in life he was especially devoted to the "chase" which he followed with the same zeal and ardour that distinguished his more serious pursuits.

At the commencement of Mr. Gladstone's first ministry in 1869 he was offered his baronetcy in recognition of his support to the Liberal Party. This honour was conferred upon him by the accolade of Queen Victoria in June of that year.

In 1849 Sir Hardman purchased a portion of the Allerton Hall Estate, Liverpool and built Allerton Towers. There his wife died on 26 March 1850, aged 52 years. He then spent 27 years a widower until his death on 25 January 1877, aged 85 years. Both he and his wife are buried in Woolton Parish Churchyard.

The GOOD OLD DAYS

THE VIADUCT WAGON WORKS

On 1 March 1853, the London and North Western Railway, under the direction of Sir Hardman Earle, leased from Messrs. Jones & Potts a small works known as the Viaduct Foundry. So named for its proximity to Stephenson's famous Viaduct over the St. Helens canal on the one-time Liverpool Manchester Railway.

The circumstances of the building by Stephenson of the Liverpool Manchester Railway and its ceremonial opening on 15 September 1830, with a procession of trains hauled by a number of locomotives, one of which was Stephenson's famous "Rocket" are too well known to require repetition here, but the fact that at Rainhill, a few miles from what is now Earlestown, the locomotive trials took place, and the first railway fatality, when Mr. Huskisson M.P. was knocked down and killed by the "Rocket" on the opening day.

The accident occurring near to what is now Newton-le-Willows station serves to illustrate that the Viaduct Works is situated in the very cradle of railway history, and has been closely connected with it from its earliest days.
The Viaduct Foundry was a small engineering works set up by Messrs. Jones, Turner & Evans in 1833 and amongst other products they built at least one locomotive named "Black Diamond" for use on one of the nearby Haydock Collieries, in which Evans had a proprietary interest. Pumping machinery for the mines were also manufactured.

It had rail connections at the easterly end of the Sankey Viaduct, and it is asserted locally that the "Rocket" was serviced and watered in the works; proof of this claim is lacking, but excavations under the floor of the "Square Smithy" on the spot where the watering is said to have taken place revealed a line of stone blocks with cast iron rail chairs with chair bolts set in lead, presumably the early Liverpool Manchester permanent way, which lends colour to our heritage.

By 1853 the owners were Messrs. Jones & Potts and the works covered about eight acres and included some 33 workers' cottages, (Owen St. and Norris St.) all of which were later demolished to make way for the development of the factory under railway management. The country lane giving access to the foundry was called "Pepper Alley Lane" which was renamed Earle Street as a compliment to Sir Hardman Earle, the LNWR director whose guidance the company bought and developed the Works and whose name is also perpetuated in the name of the township built close to the Works by the railway company for the employees.

Towards the end of 1852, the locomotive shops at Crewe were inadequate for the number of repairs currently required and it was decided in January, 1853, that the Edge Hill shops, Liverpool, should concentrate wholly on locomotive work. Additional accommodation would have to be found for the operations of the Wagon Department of the Northern Division of the LNWR and negotiations were entered into with Jones & Potts.

They were prepared to lease the foundry for two years at £650 per annum or for seven years at £600 per annum. It was stated that the reward was accommodation for building 1000 wagons and 50 engines per annum and the premises to be let included "one 24 horse engine, one 18 horse engine, 40 Smiths' fires, one large hooping furnace, one foundry, three cupolas, one brass foundry, gas apparatus, one office and drawing room, warehouse, dining room for 200 men and stables for eight horses".

The tenancy was approved on 12 February 1853, and the lease of the property dated from 1 March 1853. At the end of the seven year lease the property was bought for £15,000.

LNWR PERIOD 1853-1923

Turning to the history of the years of railway ownership and recalling the growth of the Works and the activities carried on, there are three distinct phases which can be clearly discerned.

1. The period of expansion from 1853-1903 when the factory grew in size from the original small foundry to the substantially large industry of a 100 years later. This almost wholly took place under the direction of J. Watson Emmett who was the Superintendent for no less than 36 years, 1867-1903, and during which time the potential of the factory as the principal wagon manufacturing and repairing works on the LNWR was built up and consolidated.

2. The period 1903-1931 when as a completely self-contained and self-supporting works, the construction of heavy maintenance of the LNWR freight stock was continued as well as the manufacturing and maintenance of the LNWR fleet of road vehicles in the northern area.

3. The period 1931-1948 when rationalisation which followed the grouping of the Railways in 1923 resulted in the centralisation of certain types of work in the factories best suited to the policy of the LMS which radically affected the Earlestown Works.

When the foundry was taken over by the LNWR in 1853 and the additional staff was transferred from Ordsall Lane, Salford, Nr. Manchester, the expansion began, and, apart from the additional Shops which were constructed it was necessary to provide housing accommodation adjacent to the Works and so the Streets known as Chandos, Booth, Lawrence, Rathbone together with Haydock Place, Newton and Sankey Terrace were built and formed the nucleus of housing and Earlestown began to take shape. It is thought that at a later date Regent Street was built and it is presummed that these houses were constructed to replace the original cottages, built by Jones & Potts, and known as Owen Street and Norris Street.

The rapid expansion of the Works was begun by Mr. Owen Owens 1853-1867 and continued by Mr. Emmett under whom practically three quarters of the shops were built, although some of them have had several uses since that time.

To accommodate the work a new wagon shed was authorised early in 1854, on additional land which had already been purchased adjacent to the Long Smithy. By 1864 wagon production was in full swing and Mr. Owens reported production for the first half of the year was:
652 new vehicles and 180 vehicles repaired: for the second half: 529 new vehicles and 202 vehicles repaired, a total of 1,552 rail vehicles and 11 road vehicles.

The production of new vehicles varied with the orders placed on the Works which was also at the time engaged on heavy repairs to wagons and the manufacture of wheels, iron and brass castings and wrought iron parts for use at the Works and for dispatch to the repair depots in the northern district.

In the year 1867 Mr. J. Watson Emmett succeeded Mr. Owens as Works Superintendent and was faced with a wholesale reduction in the building programme resulting in 124 of the staff being discharged. Fortunately this phase was not of long duration and by the beginning of 1869 orders had been received to build 1,560 new wagons.

The pace of development is shown by the following extracts of the Minutes of the Northern Section of the Locomotive & Engineering Committee:

February 1868 *LNWR Chairman visited the works and agreed Mr. Emmett's proposal to build a new shed for the tyre press at £460. Alterations to old Smithy £300.*

8 March 1878. The low side open wagon, constructed in 1hr. 41mins. by the Wagon Makers
Left to right:
F. Harwood (Chief Foreman)
In the wagon - G. Mottram, G. Profit, Crampton, L. Sydes, J. Hatton, J. Massey (Foreman), Wills, M. Watkins, Jones, D. Owen, C. James.

October 1868	*New Spring Shop and furnace ordered.*
February 1869	*Shop heating installed to Fitting, Carpentering and Wood Machine Shops.*
January 1870	*Wheel making plant authorised.*
April 1870	*Plans for new stores authorised.*
July 1871	*Timber shed approved £7,800*
June 1872	*New Wagon Shop £8,500*

Perhaps the high-light of Mr. Emmetts time as Superintendent was the building of the low side open wagon with a single side hand brake of the wood brake block type in 1hr. 41mins. on the 8 March 1878.

The growing community and the need for some local centre for relaxation and recreation was recognised and in June 1873 plans were approved for a two-storey building to serve as a dining room for the staff on the ground floor and a library and reading room on the upper floor, to be built close to the Works. This building was opened in 1877, when the Viaduct Institute was established. The personnel of the Works contributed 1d. per week with earnings over 10/- per week and a halfpennny for those earning less.

The importance of the Earlestown works as the principal wagon works of the LNWR was recognised in 1895 when the works was visited by the International Railway Congress on 28 June.

The personnel employed in the works in 1901 was approx. 2,000 and its capacity reported at the time was 4,000 new wagons, 13,000 heavy repairs and 300 new horse drawn-vehicles of various types.

The period 1903-1923 was not remarkable for great changes, but nevertheless steady improvement took place in keeping with production requirements. About 1890 the old Griffin Hotel had been demolished (formerly Mr. Jones's House) and the new Griffin constructed in 1891 which had made way for further development at the extreme easterly end of the works. In 1913/14 the White Shop, so named because of its construction from reinforced concrete and steel was built which was a departure from tradition as the remainder of the Works was built in dull red brick.

The Institute had also increased providing recreation with three bowling greens, a first class cricket pitch, three tennis courts and an athletic track. A number of small buildings and pavilions allocated to the various sections provided adequate amenities. An outstanding feature of the Institute's activities was the pensioner's section with an excellent pavilion built in 1923 and named 'Warneford Hall' after Mr. W. H. Warneford, Works Superintendent 1916-1924.

Circa 1915. The Viaduct Institute Grounds

Circa 1920. Saw Mill

GROUPING AND NATIONALISATION

Under the grouping of Main Line Railways the LNWR became one of the constituent companies forming the London Midland & Scottish Railway.

The Works became the principal LMS factory for heavy repairs to wagons and the manufacture and repair of door to door containers of all types.

The repair of road vehicles, horse-drawn and motor was maintained and manufacture of wagon laminated springs and three link couplings for the whole system was concentrated at the Viaduct Works.

Under new management shortly after the grouping Mr. (later Sir) Ernest Lemon became Superintendent of both Earlestown Works and Newton Heath Works, Manchester. He introduced new methods of construction of wagons at Earlestown and standard wood framed open goods wagons were produced by mass production methods on a production line system. At the same time the 'Arcade' was converted into a wheel assembly and wheel dismantling shop.

In 1931 Mr. Anthony became the works Superintendent and the task fell upon him to repair wagons on progressive lines and to re-organise the Works to accommodate wagon, lorry and road motor body repair transferred from Newton Heath which took the place of new work lost at the Earlestown Works.

The progressive system was applied, necessitating the introduction of power-operated hand tools both electric and compressed air.

The thirties saw the abolition of the Stamping Shop, Bolt Shop, Forge, Rolling Mill and the Iron and Brass Foundries although there names lingered on for many years.

In October 1943 the old method of manufacturing 3-link wagon couplings by hand forging was discontinued and an electric flash-butt welding process was brought into use. The main sawmill supplied the needs of the factory and out-stations in milled timber of all descriptions. On the retirement of Mr. Anthony in 1946, Mr. A. E. Bates was appointed and made changes in Shop layouts, so that the large numbers of wagons which were standing idle awaiting repair, owing to the after-effects of the war, as well as the increasing number of steel-frame and all-steel wagons could be dealt with more expeditiously.

In 1952 the workforce was approx. 1,900 of which 1,700 were actually employed in the workshops.

It is sad to say that in 1964 the Viaduct Works closed following the controversial Beeching Report on British Railways, but many memories live on of the Works that was the very foundation of Earlestown nearly one hundred and forty years ago . . . .

Horse-drawn Parcel Collecting Van.
Constructed and repaired at the Viaduct Works.

Circa 1928. Men of the Bolt Shop. Some of the young men were only 14 years old.
*"We started work at 6 a.m. in the morning and then nipped home at 8 a.m. for our breakfast.
And all for 3/9d. per week".*
"Yes, they were Good Old Days, there was a strong spirit and good comradeship amongst a great bunch of lads".

YESTERDAYS OF A RAILWAY TOWN

I hope this section prompts you to say
*"Eh, I remember that building, so and so lived there,
it should have never been demolished . . . .
I remember it well , Earlestown is an interesting
place with a good social history".*

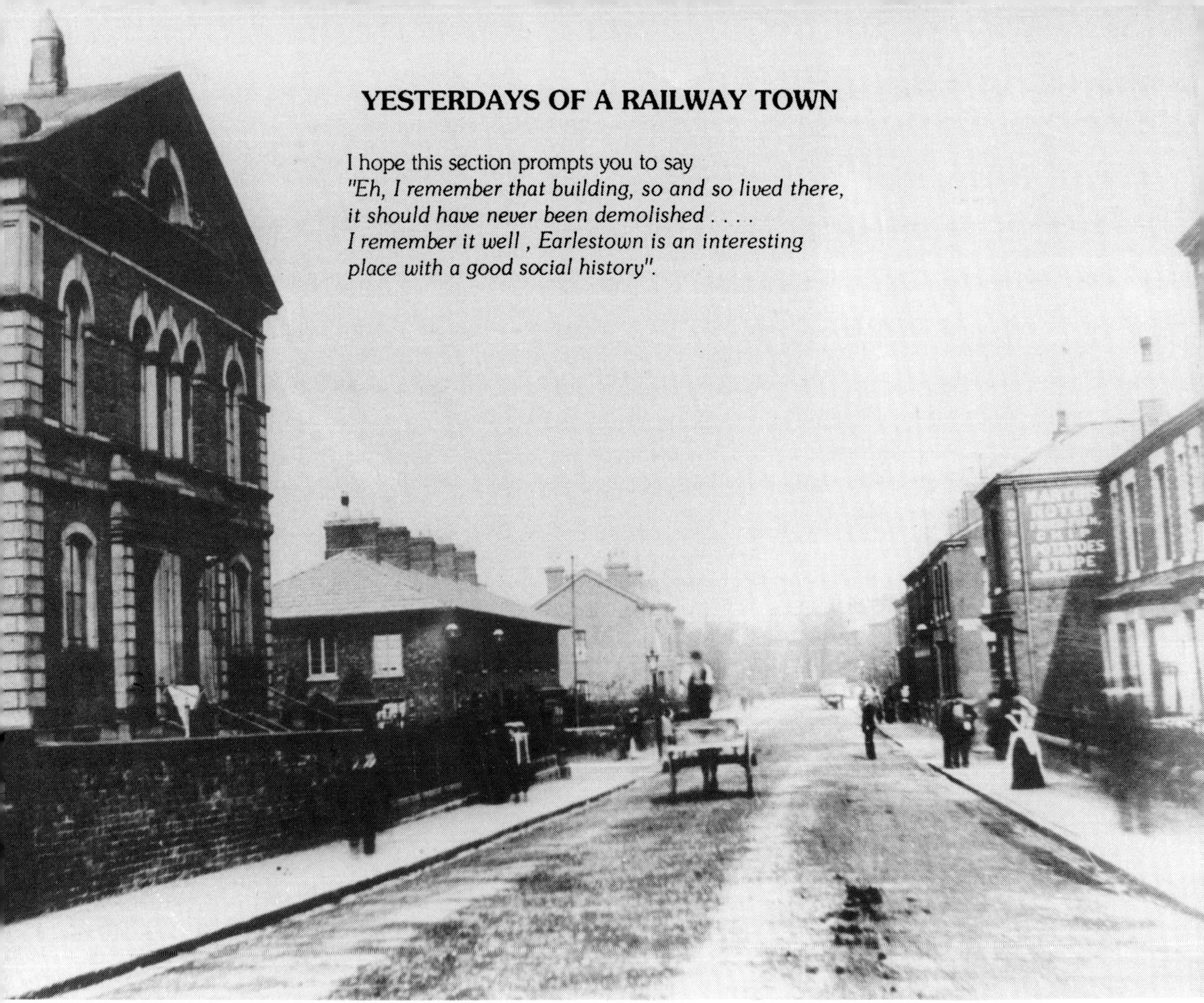

**Circa 1914. Looking down Cross Lane from the bridge.
The1880 Wesleyan Chapel is on the left and then Compensation Cottages.
On the other side of the road at the corner of Hotel Street is 'Charlie Owens' (The Royal Hotel).
On the other corner is Martins Fish and Chip Shop.
Higher up was Gilmans Cafe.**

CARAVANS.
MOTOR BODIES,
HOOP-LAS,
MADE TO ORDER.

PETROL. OILS.
TYRES IN STOCK.

COFFIN MAKER AND
UNDERTAKER.

Tel.:
176 Newton-le-Willows.

Crow Lane Carriage Works,

EARLESTOWN, NEWTON-LE-WILLOWS,
(Lancs.)

Dec 18 1936

Mrs. Hornby

Memo. from **J. Markland,**

Wheelwright, Coach Builder and General Smith.

To Panelled Oak Coffin	10·10·0
Hearse & 4 Cars.	6 10 0
Car to Cemetery	2 6
Drivers Fees. Etc.	10 0
Cemetery Fees.	12·1·4
St Johns Church	3 0
Tea at Gilmans	2 8 0
	32·4·10
	22 0 0
	£10·4·10

Cash 7-0-0
— 12 0 0
3 0 0
22·0·0

Settled with thanks Dec 1936

A funeral account from J. Markland in 1936 at a total cost of £32 4s. 10d.
The tea at Gilmans Cafe in Cross Lane cost £2 8s. 0d.

The old coal yard at the corner of Cross Lane and Haydock Street, later used as a depot for the Market stalls. It is now the site of The Post Office. Further on were two rows of terrace houses and then Stainer House which at the time of the photograph was Dr. Valentine's surgery.

Mr. Garret Ronayne was born in 1833 at Ferry Bank, County Kilkenny, near the City of Waterford. He served in No.3 Company, 3rd Bengal European Regiment and took part in the Indian Mutiny in 1857 - 1858.

As a local poet he sent seven letters and poems to His Late Majesty King Edward VII and received acknowledgement to each.

He is seen here 80 years of age, at his bungalow in Bridge Street on the day of the Royal Visit by King George V and Queen Mary in July 1913.

Courtesy of St. Helens Local History and Archives Library

At the top of Fairclough Street was Susan Forshaw's Model Lodging House . . . . I have heard it said that you could have a stand up sleep for the night on a clothes line for twopence. In the morning they undid the line to wake the clients up. . . . The premises were built before the bridge over the Colliery Line, as Fairclough Street was much higher and you looked down onto the paved yard to the front.

The Fairclough Street crossing of the Haydock Colliery Railway line over Wargrave Road. Joe Leatherbarrow is seen nearest the gate. This photograph brings back many memories, as our house, 2 King Street backed on to the line and when I was a small boy I would visit Joe's little cabin further up the line and he would let me operate the signals and play with the red and green flags.

1907. The Railway Hotel or as known to the locals 'The Bottom House'. The pub got it's nickname by the young men from the Common making it their last port of call on Saturday night drinking spree.

1903. Millards Shop Vitriol Square.
The shop was taken over later by Mr. Wallace and sold little else but bottles of pop. In the school holidays all the kids called at the shop for their pop on the way to play on the 'Muckey Mountains and in Jones's Wood'.

Courtesy of St. Helens Local History and Archives Library.

An original row of houses built by Jones and Potts in 1849 and referred to as 'The Front Row'.
Norris Street and Owen Street were at right angles to this row on the other side of Earle Street (Pepper Alley).
The shop in the centre, shown here as Peter Kenny's barbers shop, originally had iron railings round and access to a cellar.
Further down the street and three doors from the end was Wynroe's sweet and tobacconist shop, also selling papers to the Viaduct Workers.

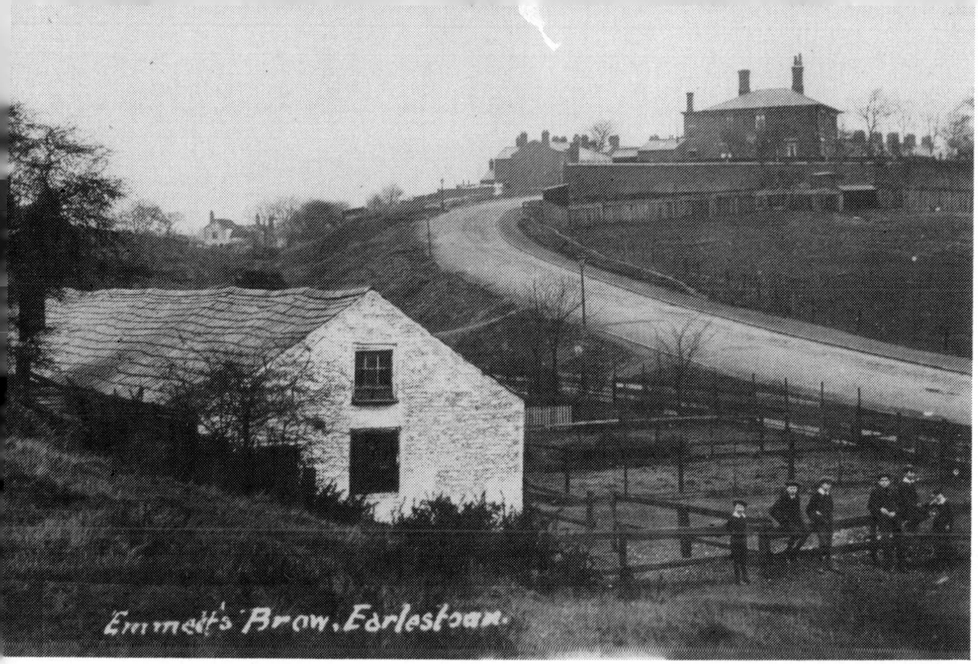

Circa 1910. Emmett's Brow.
The house at the top of the brow is Earle Cottage and was occupied by Mr. J. Watson Emmett, Superintendent of theViaduct Works, hence 'Emmets Brow'.
The cottage to the left is Stephensons Cottage were George Stephenson lived whilst building the Sankey Viaduct.

The Sankey Viaduct or as locally known as 'The Nine Arches'.
The Sankey Viaduct was completed for the opening of the Liverpool and Manchester Railway in 1830.
This is quite an historic spot for it is where the first passenger railway passed over the first industrial canal . . .
and it's at Earlestown.

Circa 1890. The Grandstand at Newton Racecourse, The Common, Earlestown. Horse racing started on The Common in 1660 and the last races were held on 13 and 14 May 1898 and then transferred to Haydock Park Race Course. The Grandstand was derelict for many years and was finally demolished in the twenties. It is said that some of the ladies from St. Philips Church chipped the old bricks for the base of their church. What a building this would have been to preserve!

The Grange. This photograph shows Grange Lodge at the bottom of the path which leads to Grange Farm and on to Haydock. I wish I had as many pounds as the number of times my grandfather and father have walked down the Grange! !

CHILDHOOD DAYS

Earlestown District Infant School.

The Earlestown District Infant School was built in1857 and stood on the site facing the Market Square.

As Earlestown began to grow it was recognised by the London North Western Railway Company that they had a responsibility to educate the children of their workers. The nearest school was the Wargrave National School on what was known at that time as 'Wargrave Moss' and concern was expressed at the danger to the children in having to cross the railway tracks to gain access to the road leading to the school.

On 6 December 1853, Mr. Owen Owens, Superintendent of the Viaduct Works submitted a plan for fitting out a room in the Works for use as a schoolroom and he referred to it as the 'Long Room'.

The Directors of the company agreed on the plan subject to it not costing more that £12 and if the room was required at some future time in connection with the purpose of manufactory it must be given up. Canon John Whitley, Rector of Newton, submitted a report on 7 August 1856, advising the railway company that the population had risen from 500 to 2,000 and there was neither School nor School House nor Reading Room in the developing area of Newton (Earlestown). The directors agreed that a school should be built and Mr. Legh, Lord of the Manor, presented a very suitable piece of ground valued at £200. Mr. Thomas Stone, a local builder, drew up plans for the school and it is decribed as: *"The dimension of the school rooms are to be 48ft long; 30ft wide; height 28ft to ridge, 12 ft to the underside of Tye beam. One classsroom 19ft 8in x 17ft 10in; one classsroom 9ft 8in x 13ft. A residence for a teacher with a parlour, kitchen and scullery with bedrooms over".*

The total cost of the building of the school was £1,521 7s. 2d. and contributions to the fund came from grants and gifts from the railway company, Mr. Legh, Lord Derby and Canon Whitley. On the opening of the school in May 1858 there was a short fall of £303 and Canon Whitley had the task of raising the money. It appears that the problem was overcome by the generosity of the schools first managers. The railway company contributed £25 per annum to the school and the scholars had to pay 1d. weekly for their instruction.

The first Mistress of the school was Margaret McDonald 1857-1860 and the 1st year Pupil Teachers, M. E. Owen and E. Williams instructed the children in the three 'R's'. By 1890 the school was not large enough to accommodate all the children of the area so in August 1891 the District Junior School was opened on the site adjoining the Infant building.

Due to further expansion of the Town 1895-1915 the Manor School and Lyme Infants School were built to accommodate the increase in the number of children in 'The Common' area.

An artist drawing of the1857 Infant Building and School House is taken from plans drawn by Thomas Stone. The plaque over the front door was inscribed 'Earlestown District Infant School 1857'.

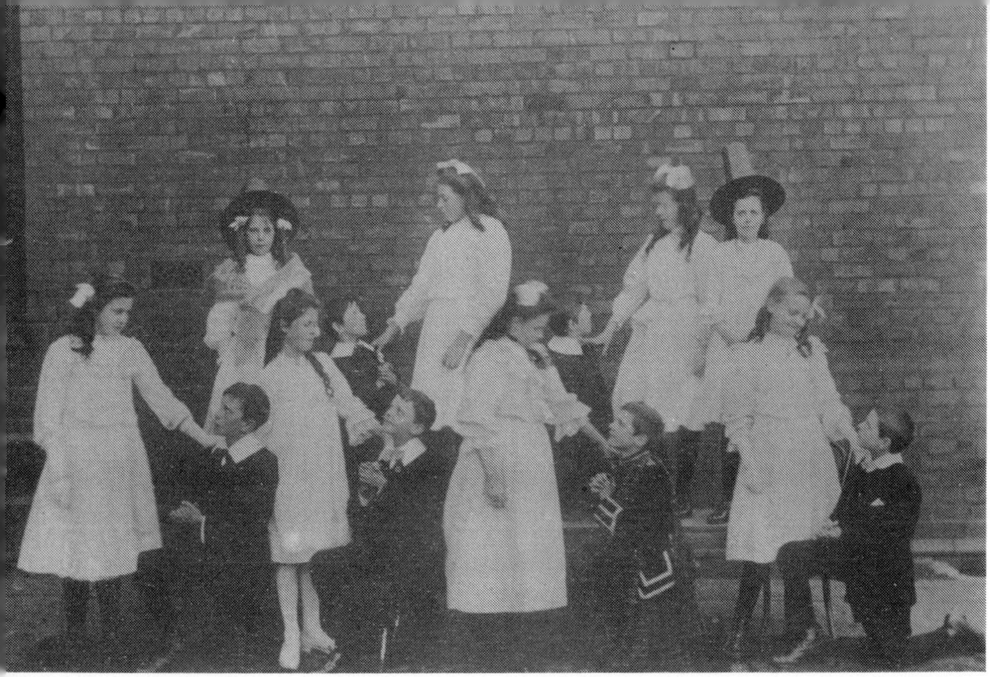

Circa 1908. C. H. Dawson's Choir at the District School. The boys were singing *"Tell me pretty maiden are there any more at home like you?"*

Circa 1909. Junior Class at the District Junior School.
The schools first Headmaster, Mr. Alec Brown, affectionately known as 'Cockey' Brown, is on the left of the photograph, and the teacher to the right is Mr. Stringer.

Notice the Honours Board on the sliding screen.

1920. District School.
Dolly Welsh's class pose for the photographer during a reading lesson.

1921. Manor C of E School,
Standard 2 Class.
Front row left to right:
Evelyn Rowbottom, Emma Holland, Mable Poulson, Maggie Irving, Louise Gorse.
2nd row: Phoebe Balmer, Fred Edwards, Bill Thomas, Cliff Ashcroft, Jack Richard, Maggie Hill.
3rd row: Ethel Smallshaw, Jim Taylor, Nellie Parkin, Bob Jones, Marie Falstead, Fred Greenhall, Danny Crooks.
Side row: Bessie Lawton, Ted Higginson, Ada Irving, Ethel Brown, Les Corless.
Mr. G. Collinge, Headmaster and Mrs. Birchall, Teacher.

Edith Emily Hornby was born in August 1901 and lived at 79 Regent Street and attended the District School.
The photograph shows her at the age of twelve in her Sunday best clothes which she wore first for Walking Day.

1914. The Kenning Family originated from Regent Street.
Left to right: Ted, Mrs. Kenning, Mr. Kenning, Frank and W. H. 'Billy' Kenning.
This photograph is a typical family group that would be taken by Earlestown's local photographer Rowland King and shows the dress of the day.

1923. Ellen and Lily Wood of Regent Street.
Lily recalls today . . . .
"Saturday night was bath night in the big tin bath on the rug in front of the fire. Then you had rags put in your hair to make it curl.
Up early Sunday morning and then went to Sunday School at the Iron Mission Hall at the bottom of Legh Street which belonged to St. Johns Church.
We used to play shop and make mud pies and our money was different coloured pieces of pot and glass . . Happy Days . . . ."

The Lythgoe Children from Wood Street.
The push chair is contructed of wood and they are wearing shining cloggs . . . .

Earlestown had many families that had moved in to the town from Wales for work.
We see here Margaret Ball and Gwen Simm in their traditional Welsh costume as representative girls from the Welsh Baptist Sunday School, Clarence Street on Walking Day.

1937. Chandos Street Party celebrating the Coronation of King George VI and Queen Elizabeth.

1948. A Baby Show in Earlestown. I wonder who won ! !
No doubt every mother thought her child should have taken 1st prize.

OUR CHRISTIAN HERITAGE

'Whatsoever thy hand findeth to do, do it with all thy might".
Eccles 9.10

WESLEYAN METHODISM

The Weslyan Methodist Church at Earlestown was formed by a few men, who were staunch Wesleyans from Salford, being transferred from the Ordsall Lane Wagon Works to the Viaduct in 1853. They had only been in the town a week or so when they set about organising a Methodist cause and devotional week-night meetings were held in the home of Mr. Joseph Atkinson. The first meeting was held on 20 November 1853 and on a Sunday they journeyed to the Wesleyan Chapel at Burtonwood for preaching services.

This practice was followed for a few weeks until 'The Long Room' at the Viaduct Works became available. On the 1 January 1854 it was opened for regular preaching services, the preacher being Mr. Joseph Hewitt of Prescot, and his text was *"Whatsoever they hand findeth to do, do it with all they might"*.

After the Long Room had been occupied for some years it was found inconvenient to the Railway Company for services to be continued there and the congregation was moved to part of the Viaduct Works Paint Shop. Eventually it was found to be undesirable to have the Works open on a Sunday and a further move was made to the Glass Bottle Works off Crow Lane.

In these three places the pioneers of the cause found their home for 13 years. During the last two years great efforts were made to build a Chapel. In 1866 the building of the old Chapel in Cross Lane was commenced but the work was accompanied by such disaster that men of little faith would have been dismayed.

These setbacks included such things as the failure of the original contractor, the giving way of the foundations and the total collapse of the western gable end during a fierce gale.

Eventually, however, the top stone was put on and on the 18 January 1867 the Chapel was opened by the Rev. Richard Roberts of London. The building consisted of two rooms, the upper one being used for Sunday Services and the lower one for the Sunday School. Before long, the Wesleyans decided to open an elementary day school in the lower room of the Chapel on 6 February 1871. The denominational school continued for a period of over forty years providing education to children who were Nonconformists. Mr. Geo. Burgess was the first headmaster and the school closed when the Council School was built in Patterson Street.

From the beginning of the day school, the number of scholars steadily increased, Mr. J. W. Emmett, the Superintendent of the Viaduct Works took a great interest in its progress and welfare and by the end of the seventies the requirements of the school demanded more room.

The accommodation of the chapel was also becoming inadequate and it therefore became necessary to consider the question of a larger building. The result was to build a new larger Chapel and to use all the existing Chapel for the day school.

The new Chapel, providing accommodation for 750 Worshippers, was opened in June 1880.

The strenuous and enterprising activities of the Wesleyan Methodists described above were an expression of the fervour of the spiritual life of the Church from the time of its inception to the early years of the present century and this was shown also by the large congregations which gathered Sunday by Sunday.

Circa. 1906
The Teaching Staff of the Wesleyan Day School.
Mr. Geo. Burgess Headmaster is seated in the centre on the middle row.

PRIMITIVE METHODISM

Primitive Methodism originated in Staffordshire,and nationally they bacame known as 'Ranters'. The leaders were Hugh Bourne and William Clowes and was introduced into Earlestown by Mr. John Clarke. He came to reside in the town having been transferred along with others to the Viaduct Works from Salford. On arriving in the town in October 1853 he found many zealous and enthusiastic friends and decided to hold Camp Meetings in the open-air.

A Society was then formed consisting of John Clarke, William Prescott, Richard Reid and Thomas Brearton and services were held in Mr. Brearton's house in Earle Street. As the Society grew they moved to another house in Bridge Street which had been formed from the old Workhouse. It was soon found, however, that this room was quite inadequate to accommodate the number of worshippers and it was decided to ask the Lord of the Manor to lease a plot of land on which to build a little Chapel. This request was absolutely refused. Nothing daunted, a deputation was appointed to see The Lord of the Manor and they journeyed to Lyme Park, Disley, and successfully sought a personal interview with Mr. Legh, who, after much pleading by the deputation, granted a piece of land in Legh Street. It was, however, only granted on the condition that the building be erected in the form of two cottages, with a large room over the lower rooms. The offer was gladly accepted and the members quickly set to work. Joseph Johnstone drew the plans, other members with pick and spade dug the foundations and a number of wagon makers from the Viaduct Works did most of the woodwork. The building being finished was duly opened in 1863.

Although but a few years elapsed since the 'Prims' became the happy possessors of a meeting place, they soon found that larger premises were required and in 1872 a new Chapel, adjoining the cottages, was opened.

Circa. 1914
Primitive Methodist Church,
Legh Street.

The photograph shows the 1872 Chapel with part of the original cottages to the left and the Schoolroom at the rear

Courtesy of St. Helens Local History and Archives Library.

Further extensions to their premises was required for the Sunday School and a commodious schoolroom was opened in 1884 at the rear of the Chapel and abutting on to Lord Street.

In 1932 the Wesleyan, Primitive and United Methodist Church nationally joined together to form The Methodist Church. In 1967 the two Methodist Societies in Earlestown amalgamated and worshipped as one Society in the Cross Lane Chapel. Sadly the (1880) Chapel was demolished a few years ago. To quote John Betjeman '*It is not carved stones, nor screen or beautiful altars, nor lofty arcades, nor gilded canopies, but the men and women who minister and the people who worship that makes a church strong".*

WELSH PLACES OF WORSHIP

The origin of the Welsh places of worship is traceable to Mr. Owen Owens, the Superintendent of the Viaduct Works, who allowed his fellow Welshmen to worship in their own language in an upper room at the Viaduct Works. The congregation included members of the various Nonconformist sects, but after a few years the Congregationalists separated and opened their own Chapel, in 1865, in Houghton Street.

The Calvinistic and Wesleyan Methodists continued to worship together in the old room for some years, but as alterations at the Works necessitated the pulling down of the building the worshippers had to find new premises.

The Calvinistic Methodists in 1873 erected a Chapel in Tamworth Street at a cost of £600. The Welsh Wesleyans occupied an old blacksmith's shop in Oxford Street, where they remained for three months, having to quit because the building could not be used for the purpose of worship. In 1872, they went to Mr. Israel Jones's house in Legh Street, where they remained for three years.

By this time the Primitives had built their new Chapel and their old one, over the cottages, was let to the Welsh Wesleyans. Whilst worshipping there they accumulated a small fund and in July 1887 they opened a Chapel at the junction of Market Street and Tamworth Street.

The Welsh Baptists started their cause in 1902 in a house in Clarence Street but by 1950 all the Welsh Chapels had closed.

The Welsh contingent in the town will well be remembered for their singing and for many years held Eisteddfods in the Town Hall.

Circa 1900. The United Mens Choir of the Welsh Chapels.

THE BAPTIST CHURCH

In 1875 the Myrtle Street Baptist Church, Liverpool, came to the aid of the local Baptists, when the active Mission Committee of the Church led by Rev. Hugh Stowell -Brown added the cause at Earlestown to its list of aided Churches. At that time local Baptists held their services in a room in Market Street and then moved to the Co-operative Hall in Earle Street. As the membership grew a Chapel in 1881 was erected in Crown Street and in 1897 a schoolroom and primary rooms were added.

THE SALVATION ARMY

The Salvation Army's first Citadel was in King Street and when The Welsh Calvinistic Methodists vacated their Chapel in Tamworth Street, the Army took over the building.

The Singleton Family, all Salvationists, lived next door to the Citadel.

BRUNSWICK ROAD TOWN MISSION

In 1875 Mrs. Josiah Evans, of The Heyes, Haydock asked the Manchester City Mission to send a missionary to preach in a tent she had erected at the bottom of Legh Street, Earlestown. It was a wooden, circular structure with a canvas roof. Various missionaries came and Mr. George Dring was sent in 1885 and that cause is still known today by many of Earlestown's residents as 'Dring's Mission'.

In 1901 a new Mission Hall was opened in Brunswick Road and sadly in 1910 Mr. George Dring passed away aged 58. His son Albert was appointed to succeed his father and continued in mission work till in October 1911 Mr. and Mrs. Bimson were appointed to take over.

Circa 1908. Brunswick Road Town Mission Bible Class. Mr. Geo Dring is seated third from the left and his son, Albert is standing in the middle row, third from the right.

Owing to a doctrinal dispute with the Mission Committee Mr. and Mrs. Bimson left the Mission in 1914, and formed the Holiness Mission in Haydock Street. The appointment of a new missionary was regularly raised at almost every Committee Meeting, finally in 1926 the Manchester City Mission sent a Deaconess, Sister Hughes and she remained in post till 1935. The Mission continued until 1967 under the guidance of Mr. J. E. Kenyon.

Circa 1927. Sister Hughes at the Harvest Festival Services in the Mission Hall Brunswick Road.

HOLINESS MISSION

Circa 1915. The opening of the Holiness Mission Haydock Street.
Mr. and Mrs. Bimson are under the banner 'Holiness unto the Lord'.

EARLESTOWN PARISH CHURCH

ST. JOHN THE BAPTIST

Circa 1910.
St. Johns Church, Market Street.
The postcard shows
Rev. Thomas Matthews,
the exterior of the Church prior to the tower being built, and an internal view of the chancel.

Canon Whitley, Rector of Newton-in-Makerfield, recognised that the population of Earlestown was growing and there was a need for their own Parish Church. On 27 May 1874, Canon Whitley, called a meeting. There were present Mr. F. Harwood, and the Church Wardens of Newton-in-Makerfield Parish Church (Emmanuel Church, Wargrave). As a result it was decided to proceed with the building of a new church in the Earlestown area.

On Wednesday, 4 August 1875, the foundation stone was laid by Mrs. W. J. Legh, wife of the Lord of the Manor, who had donated the land in Market Street. The new Church was consecrated by Rt. Rev. Kelly, Assistant Bishop of Chester, on 6 January 1879. The original plans for the Church were drawn up by Messrs. Whitley & Fry of Dover and they produced a design for a building in Early English style to seat 900 persons and costing £16,000. However, their plans had to be curtailed due to lack of money and a building to seat 600 was built, leaving the remaining portion for a future effort. In 1878, the Rev. Thomas Matthews came to Earlestown, as Curate-in-Charge and on the opening of the new Church he became the first Vicar of Earlestown, a position he held till 1914.

The second effort of completion of the Church came about in the twenties when the architect's dreams had to compromise with finance and the partly-completed tower as we see it today was built onto the end of the church.

ST. PHILIPS MISSION CHURCH,

NEWTON COMMON

The population of Earlestown began to spread over on to the Common area, largely as result of the mining industry in that part of the town. In 1913, the new district of St. Philips was formed, and services were held in the Manor School.

A temporary Church and Hall were built in 1916 and a new Church was intended. Owing to various circumstances, particularly the fact that housing could not be built in the area owing to mining subsidence. St. Philips remained a Mission Church in the care of the Vicar of St. John's.

1930. The Choir at St. Philips, Newton Common.
Back row left to right: Kay, Len Clough, Bob Hill, Sam Griffiths, John Griffiths.
Middle row: Forshaw, Tickle, F. Dean, Boyes, Pendlebury, Ernie Lawton.
Front row: John Mitchell, Mr. Rothwell (organist), Rev. Thomas Lever, T. Lawrence.

CHURCH OF CHRIST

The Church of Christ began their meetings in the room over the shops adjoining Legh Street, Grant Street and Wellington Street. After a few years they moved into the former Salvation Army Citadel in King Street.

In 1926 they opened their present building on the junction of Heather Brae and Crow Lane. Mr. A. R. Phillips, of Liverpool, was the preacher for the day.

1926. The opening of the church in Heather Brae. The old lady seated is Mrs. Syarett.

ST. PATRICK'S ROMAN CATHOLIC CHURCH

In 1931 Archbishop Downey decided that it was time for St. Mary's Parish, Newton, to be divided and a new parish be formed to serve the Earlestown people.

The present site at the corner of Common Road and Marian Avenue was purchased, and work was begun. Father William Rylance was appointed the new Parish Priest and he probably chose the name St. Patrick because the Irish National Club was in the confines of the parish and a large percentage of Irish people, particularly in the Legh Street area, reside within the new parish boundaries.

The new church was a semi-permanent building and cost £2,500 to erect. Ideal weather favoured the opening ceremony on Sunday, 10 July 1932 by Archbishop Downey, when over 3,000 people swarmed on the Common to hear the speeches relayed by loud speakers.

The meeting was opened by Fr. Rylance and thanked everyone who had helped to build the church and subscribed to its furnishings.

Special thanks was expressed to the unemployed who had worked with pick and spade to make the grounds presentable for the opening day.
Archbishop Downey, who received a great ovation, expressed great joy that the new church had been erected having been contemplated for over 30 years.

The early years of parish life at St. Patrick's were happy and successful, and in 1940 Fr. Rylance was succeeded by Fr. Edward Stephens who served the parish well during the dark days of war when so many of the men were away on active service.

Circa 1940. The Roman Catholic Church of St. Patrick and Presbytery, Common Road.

WALKING DAYS

Dedicated to Percy Wolfe 1901-1986.
In recognition of his service to the United Sunday Schools Association

The Nonconformist Walking Day at Earlestown first began in 1894. "Why did it start?" is an interesting question. In the period 1880 - 1891 the Viaduct Wagon Works expanded and many wagon workers and their families came from Newton Heath, Manchester for employment. It is likely that they used their influence in the Earlestown Free Churches for a Walking Day to be established a tradition which was held in Manchester every Whit Monday.

The day commenced by the children assembling at their various Sunday Schools and arriving at the Market Ground by 9.30 a.m., where two hymns were sung. They then paraded through the main streets and returned to the Market Ground for the singing of another hymn followed by the Doxology. The children returned to their Sunday Schools for tea and sports events held on local farmers' fields.

On the afternoon of Whit Sunday, all the scholars met on alternate years in the Wesleyan and Congregational Churches to practise the hymns for the service on the following day. The nonconformist walks continued in great strength until they were abandoned owing to the commencement of the First World War in 1914.

In 1919 the Newton-in-Makerfield Sunday Schools Association was formed for the purpose of arranging the United Demonstration with the day being changed from Whit Monday to the third Saturday afternoon in June.

The Association comprised of the schools from the following churches:- All Saints, Baptist, Welsh Baptist, Brunswick Road Town Mission, Church of Christ, Congregational, St. Johns, St. Phillips, Salvation Army, Primitive Methodist, United Welsh (Congregational and Wesleyan), Wesleyan Methodist.

The first secretary and treasurer was Mr. Harry Gray. In 1920 there were a total of 3,035 scholars walking, probably the highest number ever.

The United Walk became an annual event in the lives of the people of Earlestown and was of great splendour, the main street and the Market Square being full to capacity with both walkers and spectators.

The Earlestown Viaduct Band gave loyal service to the procession and led every walk from 1894 to 1960. The walks continued without a break until 1940 when again they had to be abandoned owing to the country being at war again.

In 1946 the United Walking Day recommenced and continued until 1971. At the committee meeting held on 1 April 1949 it was agreed that the route be amended from previous years, which had been around the Earlestown area only.

The new route agreed upon was Market Street, Crow Lane West, Crow Lane East, Victoria Road, Wargrave Road, Railway Street, Queen Street, Market Street and Stanley Street.

There are far too many names to mention who gave years of service to the arrangements of Walking Day. However, it is fitting to pay tribute to Tom Green, Secretary from 1948 - 1962 and to the late Percy Wolfe, Treasurer from 1948 - 1966, to whom this section of the book is dedicated. Both their Minute and Account Books are still in existence which clearly demonstrate their years of devotion to Sunday Schools in Earlestown.

Circa 1910. The procession passing the Co-op Butchers in Earle Street.

1908. The Salvation Army passing the old Police Station in Market Street. Unlike the other schools in the walk they had their banner fixed to a horse and cart. For those who have carried the banners over the years . . . . . what a good idea ! ! !

Circa 1910. Brunswick Road Town Mission parading in Earle Street.

1920. Six of the Banners on the Market Square.
Notice the Viaduct Lorries carrying the smaller children.

1920. Viaduct Band, Representative Girls, two from each school, Earlestown Baptist Church Banner. Passing the Co-op, Wellington Hotel and Smiths Fish and Chip Shop in Earle Street.

1924. The procession leaving the Market Square returning to their schools for tea.

Programme 1931. Notice all the officials wore rosettes.

NEWTON-IN-MAKERFIELD

United Sunday Schools Association.

Twelfth Annual

- United Sunday Schools -

DEMONSTRATION

ON SATURDAY, JUNE 20TH, 1931.

PRESIDENT: Mr. E. DODD (Blue and White Rosette).

VICE-PRESIDENTS: Mrs. J. HODKINSON and Mr. HARRY GRAY (Purple Rosettes).

SECRETARY AND TREASURER: Mr. FRED HAMBLETT (Orange Rosette).

EXECUTIVE COMMITTEE:—

Mr. W. Liversage	Mr. J. Bray
,, J. D. Collins	,, G. F. Barnes
,, W. Ellis	,, J. Howard
,, A. Edwards	Miss N. Seddon
,, Dyson	,, L. Smith.

CHIEF MARSHALS (Pale Blue Rosettes).

Mr. C. P. Audley	Mr. D. Clarke
,, C. Ball	,, W. Davies
,, T. Martindale	,, J. T. Clary.

CYCLE MARSHALS (Red Rosettes).

Mr. J. T. Barr	Mr. T. Edwards.

SCHOOL MARSHALS (White Rosettes).

Mr. E. Hamblett	Mr. W. Houghton
,, T. Jones	,, T. Bartley
,, W. J. Smith	,, R. J. Parry
,, G. Cruickshank	,, J. B. Wilson

Mr. A. Bonsor.

1929. Mr. William Heyes with a Viaduct Lorry carrying children from St. Phillips Sunday School.

E. T. EVANS & SONS'

EVERYTHING FOR WALKING DAY!

SEE WINDOWS FOR SPECIAL DISPLAY OF

Ladies' Frocks, Two & Three Piece Costumes, Coats, Swagger Coats, Raincoats, Blouses, Millinery, Etc.

Ladies' Linen Costumes from 18/11 Swagger Coats from 29/9

SMART DISPLAY of . . Children's Frocks & Hats for WALKING DAY.

Children's Ankle Socks from 5d pr. Silk Frocks from 3/11½

SPECIAL SHOW of . . .

Gent.s', Youths' & Boys' **Sports Wear**

Gent's TUNIC SHIRTS (with collar attached) at 3/11½ newest design
New stock of Men's TWEED CAPS at - - - 1/- & 1/6
Newest designs in Gent's SPORTS COATS & FLANNEL TROUSERS
Gent's RAINCOATS (silk lined) from 21/-. Lightweights from 5/-
Boys' Tweed SPORTS 2-PIECE SUITS, all sizes from 9/11 each
Boys' FLANNEL SUITS from - - - - 3/11½ each

Advert from E. T. Evans & Sons 1935.

1937. The Church of Christ leaving the Market Square. The District School is in the background.

1937. Brunswick Road Town Mission with their Faith, Hope and Charity Banner.

1946 DARK SKIES

An extract from the Earlestown Guardian.

"Dark skies, rain bouncing off the pavements and easily the wettest day of the year, greeted the first post-war Walking Day. Little children who had never seen or taken part in the procession clutching their baskets of flowers and with their pretty dresses covered by rain coats, hurried through the rain towards their Sunday Schools, ever hopeful that the sun would force its way through the heavy sky.

A meeting of the executive committee was held shortly after one o'clock and the question of whether to postpone or cancel the walk entirely was wrestled with. To cancel would have meant doing so for the first time in the twenty-one years that it had been held.

Some members remembered another occasion when the walk was delayed until the evening, when the weather cleared and it was an outstanding success. Although there was not a break in the sky the committee agreed to adjourn till five o'clock and in the meantime the kiddies were given their tea indoors.

The rain eased shortly before five o'clock and the sun made a valiant break through. The committee agreed that the walk should take place at six o'clock, providing it was fine ! ! !

Cycle Marshalls toured the schools giving the secretaries the decision and shortly after 5.30 p.m., although it was still raining, the various schools began to assemble on the Market Square. Banners, Bands and Happy smiles challenged the leaden skies, although with most of the processionist umbrellas and macs were still the dress of the day.

The hymn Fight the Good Fight conducted by Mr. W. H. Kenning was the prelude for the procession leaving the Market Square on a much curtailed route.

A two and half year old Pauline Robinson, probably the youngest flower girl to walk, seemed to be enjoying it most of all. To the delight of hundreds of spectators Pauline with her basket of flowers which was nearly as big as herself, practically danced the whole of the route. Pauline who whilst waiting for the procession to disperse, said to her Mother "Again! Again!"

Mr. J. T. Barr, a Cycle Marshall, every year since he was fourteen was busier than ever and got wetter than ever dashing from school to school."

It was Banners, Bands and Happy smiles all the way!!

1948. Legh Street Methodist Primary.

MARKET AND SHOPPING DAYS

THE MARKET AND THE OBELISK....

As a recognised market town, Newton-in Makerfield was of importance many years ago for we read that after the execution of King Charles (30 Jan, 1649) and the transformation of the Monarchy into a Commonwealth, proclamation was issued that whosoever should proclaim a new King without the authority of Parliament should be deemed a traitor and it was ordered to be read in every market town.

It was read at Newton on 9 February, 1649 at 3.00 p.m. as it appears from Sheriff's return to the Speaker of the House of Commons.

The Newton Market and Fairs were originally held along High Street, Newton, and were transferred to the Earles town Market Ground on 31 August, 1870, when the market rights were leased by Mr. Legh (Later Lord Newton) to the Newton Improvement Commissioners.

The land which forms the present Market Square and the site of Stainer House (now demolished) was previously used by Thomas Bethell as a brickyard. The clay was extracted from the site beside the Haydock Colliery Railway and the flats and kilns being on the square. The opening of the Market Ground was commemorated by sports events on the adjoining land (now Haydock Street and Stanley Street) farmed at the time by Mr. Pearce.

Markets, along with other events, have been held there ever since on the square. The wooden stalls were illuminated by unprotected naphtha lamps to provide lighting till late in the evening on Market day. Horse-drawn vehicles brought shoppers to the open market from surrounding towns of Ashton, Golborne and Lowton.

Circa 1930. The Market and The Obelisk

When the stalls were not required, they were stored in a wooden structure called the Alexandra Theatre built by George Bailey which was also used as a place of amusement on weekdays and for religious services on Sundays.

In 1883 it was crowded to suffocation when a benefit was given to Bob Carlisle following his successful accomplishment of a self-imposed task of walking 2,000 miles in 1,000 hours. The last 600 miles were walked around Earlestown Market Square.

Sangers Circus used to visit the town every few years. Massey's shooting gallery, Martin's canvas pea salon and Greenwoods auction tent have all stood on the market ground. Greenwoods tent was also used for boxing competitions, and so was nicknamed 'The Blood Tub'.

Mr. Kemp, before he built his cinema in Chemical Street also had a tent showing pictures. Apparently the canvas was like a colander and patrons spent more time moving about avoiding the rain than watching the silent pictures. Music was provided by a pianist and a big carrot was your refreshment.

THE OBELISK
"Better known to Earlestonians as 'The Milly Stone'"

The Milly Stone was first erected in 1818 in the church yard at St. Peter's Church, Newton, to replace the wooden market cross bearing the arms of the Legh family. It is reputed to have been quarried at Lyme Park, Disley; the shaft weighs fifteen tons and the pedestal three. Reports say it took twenty horses seven days to bring it from Disley and broke several bridges on the way. Mr. Andrew Brown won the tender at £15 when it was brought from St. Peter's to Earlestown Market on 1 June, 1870. In recent times the fact that the Milly Stone came from Disley has been disputed on the basis that at Lyme Park there is no Bathstone of which the Obelisk is made.

Where it came from remains a mystery. It has been a landmark in Earlestown for over a hundred and twenty years..... long may it remain so!

"The Milly Stone" was a popular place for children to meet and to play on the steps.
Stainer House is seen in the background.

Courtesy of St. Helens Local History and Archives Library.

The Main Shopping Streets in Earlestown are Market Street, Bridge Street and Queen Street. The photograph is looking up Market Street from the junction with Bridge Street.
The Town Hall clocktower is in the background.

Circa 1900. Bridge Street. Looking down from Cross Lane Bridge. Originally this was part of Pepper Alley.
The three storey building in the photograph is Freeman, Hardy and Willis, Shoe Shop.
No Yellow Lines or Traffic Wardens!!

MARKET STREET

E. T. EVANS and Sons . . . The Harrods of Earlestown

E. T. Evans was born in 1831 at Llandudno and came to Earlestown as manager and partner of Evans and McLure, Drapers at 1 Bridge Street.

In 1871 he left the partnership and founded his own business of Draper and Outfitter at 21 and 23 Market Street. Later he expanded his business into house furnishings at premises across the street (now Woolworth's).

He was eventually joined in the business by his two sons, Alec and Robert, with branches opening in Nelson 1881, Haydock 1882 and Ashton 1897. E. T. Evans attended the Welsh Calvinistic Methodist Church in Tamworth Street. In 1890 he was elected a Member of the Board of Commissioners and to the newly formed Urban District Council in 1895, representing the Town Hall Ward, a position he held unopposed. By 1906 he had been appointed a Justice of the Peace and took a very active role in the well being of the Town.

He died in May 1913 and is buried in the Newton Cemetery.
His wife Lucy, a native of Richmond, Yorkshire died in March 1914.

The business continued until 1949-1950 when the premises were sold to the Earlestown Co-op, following the death of his last surviving son.

Circa 1905. E. T. Evans 21 and 23 Market Street

"My aunt Maggie had a lovely three piece suite in the parlour which came from E.T.'s, of course you only sat on it on special occasions. It was a ton weight".

"My father's mother lived in Earle Street, she made union shirts for E.T. Evans but my mother did the button holes.
I would go with grandma to take the shirts. They were all wrapped up in brown paper. That was over 85 years ago".

Circa 1900. The staff of E. T. Evans with the founder seated in the centre of the second row. The man to the right of E. T. is Mr. Spottiswood who ran the curtain department.

Circa 1895. E. T. Evans delivery cart and horse. It would appear from the lettering on the cart items were taken in part exchange. You can also see the three brass balls of the Pawnbroker, next door. Why three brass balls? Two to one you don't get your money back! ! !

The staff and friends of E. T. Evans on a coach trip to Southport in 1929.
Front row (left to right):
John Conheeny, Elsie Drummond, Mrs. Williams, Agnes McLeish, friend, Ethel Kynaston, Miss Harvey, Mr. & Mrs. Thomas (standing).
Second and back row:
Mary McGloughlin, Driver, Betty Rothwell, Miss Higgins, friend, Phyllis Powell, Miss Smith, Essie Briscoe, Mrs. Rhodes, Madge Rayner, Hilda Clarke, Miss I. Baxter.

Circa 1910. Cash Clothing Company, 32 Market Street
The manager, W. B. Hornby, is standing in the doorway of the shop. The dummy to the left is displaying a suit at a price of 12/-
Billy Hornby, as he was known, later opened his own gents outfitters in Wellington Street and on the opposite side of the road he had a toffee shop.
"I would go into Hornby's from the District School to spend my Friday penny. I would get a bag of sherbert and a stick of spanish. There was a big mirror on the shop wall so they could see from the back room who came into the shop".

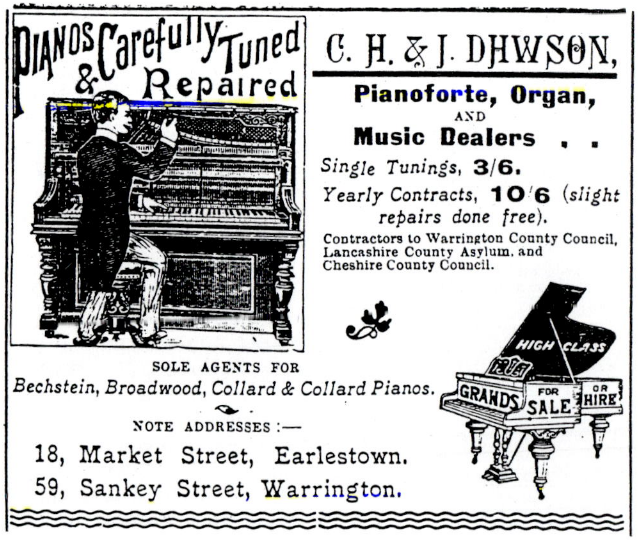

Advert 1910

Liza Lovesey in her younger days.

Circa 1920. Lovesey's, Greengrocer and Florist, 26 Market Street.
The photograph shows Ma Busby and John Crompton outside the shop in Market Street. The sign indicates that the business was established in 1885.
"Ma Busby was well known for curing warts. She had a secret paste and when you called in the shop for treatment you stood behind her with your arm under hers so you could not see what she was using on your hand . . . .
She cured my sister's warts when all other treatments had failed".

Liza Lovesey, Ma Busby's sister, was born in 1873 and was a well known character about town. She took over the fish and fruit round from her brothers, Johnny and Charlie.
She wore a large sack apron and a man's flat cap and could be heard streets away shouting *"Finney haddy"* from her horse and cart.
In later years she had a little shop in her parlour at 47 Legh Street and sat at the middle door waiting for customers to come in.
She died in October 1951 aged 78.

Circa 1900. Charlie Lovesey in Crown Street with his horse and cart.
The horse was called *"Tommy"* and sadly went blind.

BRIDGE STREET

Circa 1910. Peter Thompsons, Grocers, at the corner of Bridge Street and Haydock Street.
This photograph shows Tom Gregory (left) when he was the Manager, with Jim Anders. He later took over the business and was joined by his two sons, John and Arthur. They ran a very well respected grocers and Ceros Bakeries.
In 1910 they were *"Giving away Golden Fleece Margarine at 1/- per lb."*
Notice the sides of bacon hanging outside.
"You were posh if you shopped at Gregory's, it was all the best stuff they had".

1935 John, Tom and Arthur Gregory sitting outside the shop

Circa 1930.
Tom Gregory and Sons Ltd.
The staff of the grocers and Ceros Bakeries pose for the photographer.
(left to right):
Wilf Eaton, Ellen Astall,
Alice Anderton, Mrs. Garnet,
Louie Brooks, Mary Woodward,
Harvey Burman, Fred Burman.

Circa 1900. J. A. Wild, 26 Bridge Street.
By 1907, the shop had been taken over by S. Deveraux but many Earlestown residents will remember it being run by Mr. and Mrs. Hall until quite recently.

"My dad always sent me to Hall's for an ounce of St. Bruno's. You could have some toffee with the change for going".

Peter Price outside his barber's shop in Bridge Street.
Peter, born in Haydock Place, worked as a barber all his life starting his apprenticeship as a lather boy. Both he and his wife were loyal worshippers at St. Johns Church.
A typical conversation in the shop . . . .
"Good morning Sir, haircut?'
"Good morning Peter, yes please, short back and sides and Brylcreem on top".
. . . . some had to have sandpaper ! ! !

Circa 1918. Parr's Bank, 6 Bridge Street.
In 1918, when the photograph was taken, the bank merged with London, County and Westminster, in 1923 it became known as Westminster Bank and in 1970 National Wesminster Bank. In later years the premises extended into 8 Bridge Street.

Circa 1900. Parrs Bank, corner of Bridge Street and Queen Street. The banking partnership of Jospeh Parr and Thomas Lyon, sugar refiners, and Walter Kerfoot, was established in Warrington in 1788. By 1865 it had become to be known as Parr's Bank and many branches had opened in the surrounding towns.

A branch was opened in Earlestown in August 1873, and the photograph shows the premises in c. 1900.

As the town grew and business expanded larger premises were required. The bank moved in 1904 to 6 Bridge Street which had previously been occupied by Robert Jones, Butcher.

The premises later became to be known as "Wests Corner", named after Mr. & Mrs. Claude West who kept the shop as a tobacconist.

"My father sent me to West's for his razor blades . . . . 7d. for one Ever Ready blade".

QUEEN STREET

Circa 1928. Marsdens, 38 Queen Street.
Miss Olive Marsden outside her drapers shop. She and her mother also ran a Registry Office for servants who went to work "in service".

"My sister and I both got our servants jobs at Mrs. Marsdens. You had to pay her 2/6d. for her finding you a job . . . .
mine was at a Theatre Manager's house in Bolton . . . . I was 15 at the time".

The drapers was taken over by Gladys E. Wild (Mrs. Greenslade) who moved from the Fish and Chip shop in Earle Street (next to The Wellington Hotel). Gladys ran her business for years, always had time for a chat and a friendly smile.
She is seen on the left in the photograph below.

"I got all my wool from Gladys Wilds and she was a good Councillor too"!

Circa 1930. A. P. Peake Chemist, 22 Queen Street and on the corner of Princess Street.
Mr. Peake was in business for over 50 years and was noted for Peakes Patent Healing Powder . . . .
"Mr. Peake was as good as any doctor. You'd pay a penny for a baby's teething powder . . . . it would sleep all night on it".

"If you wanted a tooth out you went to the side door in Princess Street. I was only about 9 and he took one of my back teeth out.
He nearly pulled my head off".

Circa 1928. Smith's Cafe, corner of Queen Street and Chemical Street.
Across the road from Peake's Chemist was Smith's Cafe and Sweet Shop. Miss Winifred Smith (now Mrs.W.Harvey) is standing in the door way of the cafe with her mother.
The cafe was taken over by the Co-op.

"We buried my father with a ham tea at the Co-op cafe. It was 2/9d. at the time".

Circa 1890. John Hatton, Grocer, Baker, Flour and Provision Dealer.
The premises were situated at 2 Fairclough Street at the junction with Derby Street.
Notice the cobbled street and footpath . . . .

Circa 1933. Fred Hankey, Butcher, 25 Legh Street.
(Left to right): Unknown, Fred Hankey, Maurice Hankey (in arms), Harold Hankey, George Mort and Wilf Parr.

"They sold lovely sausages at Freds".

Circa 1933. Percy Irvings Shop. The little wooden cabin was sited at the top of the 'Chicken Run' (a footpath from the top of Market Street to the Viaduct Works). Many of the Viaduct workers would call at Percy's for their cigarettes 'Gold Flake' and 'Craven A' seems to be the most popular brands, also they would get a chew of tobacco . . . .

Circa 1890. Augustus and Eliza Bethell outside their shop on the corner of Tamworth Street and Lord Street facing the side of the Town Hall.

1932. John Russells.
Russells had three shops, 1 Birch Street, 45 Athol Street and 1 Regent Street. The business was established in 1885 by John Russell's grandfather and wherever possible sold Empire produce. In addition to Bestoweat Bread they sold Danish and Irish bacon, butter, cheese and eggs.
The bakehouse was situated in Portland Street and employed fourteen workers making confectionery.

"Do you remember little Tommy Smith, he was the butcher for years in the Birch Street Shop? Always gave you good weight too."

"Yes, I can see him now scattering the sawdust on the floor".

1932. The shop at 1 Birch Street with John Russell entering his car.

Section of the Bakehouse in Portland Street.
Left to right: Ada Irving, Martha Scragg, Mrs. Jones, (chargehand) Edith Edwards, Tilly Jones, Alice York.

No. 1 Regent Street . . . .
The shop had for many years been run by Russell's. In later years it was Clough's, where you could obtain all your fishing requirements (now demolished)

This photograph shows three former well-known shops, Billy Naylor, Butchers ; Dykes, Newsagents and French Bros., Bicycle Shop, opposite the junction of Earle Street with Junction Lane and adjoining the Rams Head.
A newspaper cutting says,
"Mr. Charles Charlton, kept the newsagents shop in Earle Street which he and his wife started with £5.
"In 1916, I went to work at the shop" said Mrs. Dykes.
"I was 16 year old Nellie Herbert then: Mr. and Mrs Charlton more or less adopted me and very strict they were - I had to be in before 9.30 p.m. ! !"
Later I managed the shop and after their deaths I inherited the business. That was about 1933 and my husband and I ran it 'till 1959, when our son Norman took over".

LEISURE AND WINNING DAYS

'Entertainment, we made our own in Earlestown". says most of the old Earlestown residents.

The following selection of photographs highlights that statement. Whether it be a Pub Trip, the local Carnival or A Tea and Concert at a local Chapel is was all very much 'Home Made' to an excellent standard. Those who made the arrangement enjoyed it as much as those who bought tickets. Earlestown was also well known for its competitions, particularly in sport, and some of the photographs show various teams with their Winning Cups and Shields.

1931. The Rams Head Picnic Club, taken before their outing. Miss Isabell Sturgess, the Hotel's Licensee, is seated, with her sister, Mary, in the centre of the photograph.

**Circa. 1928. St. Philips Ladies Outing to Southport on Tommy Pott's coach.
All dressed in the latest fashion ! !**

Mr. Pillinger, the local herbalist, with his own designed 'Pedalless Bicycle' was very often seen gathering wild plants from the roadside or in the Dingle for his 'Lotions and Potions' which he sold from his shop at the bottom of Legh Street.
A story goes that A. A. Taylor's coach was travelling home from Southport and Mr. Pillinger overtook it on his bicycle.

Jack, Monty, Jim and friend on Fredericks Ice Cream Cart, down at the Canal, next to the danger sign near Wharf Road.
The prices are quite interesting, 'Choc Blocks 2d'.
I will leave you to date the photograph! ! !

Circa 1930. Earlestown Viaduct Prize Band.
Left to right:
Top Row: Jack Cairey, Norman Jones, Bob Ashton, Billy Marney, Harry Fogg, John Jackson, Vin Lewis, John Clarke, Joe Walton.
Middle Row: Harry Sherwood, Joe Hindley, Jack Allen, Reg Barcroft, Joe Whamond, Jim Wilson, Clarence Jones, Albert Mains, Fred Allen, Unknown.
Seated: Ike Dobson, Bill Williams, Wilmot Wynroe, Bill Kenyon, Fred Gee, Peter Duxbury, Unknown.
The photograph shows the band on the Viaduct Institute Ground.

Circa. 1930 Kynastons Coach Trip to Southport.
Left to right:
Back Row: Mary Ann Winders, Ellen Pagett, Ned Winders (driver), Vi Winders, Liza Winders.
Seated: Ella Pagett, Ken Pagett, Veronica Wood, Rueben Pagett, Bena Wood and Iris Winders.

Circa 1906. The Rink, Market Street, was first a Skating Rink and later became the Pavilion Cinema. It was a very popular place of entertainment and it has been known that you had to queue for over an hour for tickets for the Saturday night performances. Over the years the local Amateur Dramatics staged their shows there.

Circa. 1935. The LMS Choir with their two Winners Cups. Mr. J. R. Hughes Snr., the choir conductor, is seated in the centre of the front row.

This photograph shows the principal characters of the Newton-le-Willows Amateur Dramatic and Operatic Society's production of 'Miss Hook of Holland' in 1948 staged at the Pavilion Cinema.
Every night was a sell out! ! !

Circa 1910. The Viaduct Works Ambulance Team with three Winners Shields in the inter-works ambulance competition.

The White Star Football Club 1930.

Left to right: Sam Griffiths, Jack Pantor, Louie Corns, Joe Rogers, Harold Breaton, Gaskel Bros. Jack and Tommy.
Seated: Frank Rogers, Jack Seddon, Jack Hughes.
Front Row: Theo Myatt, Peter Ashcroft, Ted Elliott, Harold Camwell, Harold Hickey.

The Club acquired its name from the White Star Shipping Line as they supplied them with their first football shirts.
In their first season they won The Warrington League and went on to win the Starkey Cup and The Liverpool Jnr. Cup.
The club's home ground was on the Sugar Works Field, later they moved to 'Tushinghams Field' at a cost of £20 per year.
Tommy Darby was the Secretary and Ernie Townsend the Manager.

Viaduct Harriers. This photograph, possibly taken in the mid thirties, shows the runners with their Winning Cup.

Circa 1936. Swan Temperance Prizeless Band.
The Swan (Hotel) Temperance Band was well known for its appearance at local charity carnivals. Many stories abound about its performances and humour. Once they were travelling to the Winsford Carnival and the coach driver got lost, 'Bronk' got off the coach to ask a passer-by the way and she'ran a mile'. It must have been quite frightening to see a man covered in 'Coca' and wearing a grass skirt! !

One year they were winners of a Carnival Cup and it went on display in Irvings shop window (bottom shop in Birch Street) then it went missing. It turned up all battered and when they returned it to the Carnival, the Committee disqualified them from entering because of the damage to the cup.
The band's instruments and costumes were all "Home Made' a bike frame for a triangle . . . . it was all good fun ! ! ! !

Behind the make-up and the costumes are some of the men, together with their wives and families who made the real Earlestown.

"Yes, Earlestown has changed in my life-time, I wouldn't live anywhere else and I love every cracked flag".